Fathering the Fatherless

the

Fatherless

TODD JOHNSON

authorHOUSE®

AuthorHouse™
1663 Liberty Drive
Bloomington, IN 47403
www.authorhouse.com
Phone: 1 (800) 839-8640

Published by AuthorHouse 10/24/2019

Scripture quotations marked NIV are taken from the Holy Bible, New International Version®*. NIV*®*. Copyright* © *1973, 1978, 1984 by International Bible Society. Used by permission of Zondervan. All rights reserved. [Biblica]*

New King James Version (NKJV)
Scripture taken from the New King James Version®*. Copyright* © *1982 by Thomas Nelson. Used by permission. All rights reserved.*

ISBN: 978-1-7283-3314-4 (sc)
ISBN: 978-1-7283-3312-0 (hc)
ISBN: 978-1-7283-3313-7 (e)

Library of Congress Control Number: 2019917131

Print information available on the last page.

CONTENTS

DEDICATION OF THE BOOK

I DEDICATE THIS BOOK FIRST AND FOREMOST TO GOD MY Heavenly Father for always being there for me, never giving up on me or for stopping loving me no matter what.

Also to my Lord and Savior Jesus Christ, for the cross and selfless sacrifice He made for me and you.

(John 3:16)

Giving us the Holy Spirit for His guidance, direction and wisdom. Most of I dedicate it to all my treasures, my children who are the reason why I am writing this book. I aim to be the best dad I can be every day, when I wake up for my children.

INTRODUCTION

WE AS FATHERS, NEED TO REALIZE THAT WE SET OUR CHILDREN up to win or fail, to lead or fail to fight for what's right, or to give up and go astray. As a father, I want to do more than what I should.

To go above and beyond and show my kids this is what you do, live, apply, and pass on as a father. We, as fathers, must realize our words and comments are like a two edged sword that can speak life or death and blessing or curses.

We must lay down our will and put our wives and children first after God, to set the example of how to live and behave with dignity.

The problem is more at home than out in the world. If we accept and live our life lessons example our children at home, then we will have good role models and leaders in this world when we work hard.

Or crime in general? It is time to lead and set boundaries to better our children futures.

We need to let our kids know they're loved and cared for and to show them what hard work and respect are. We have to teach them that life is what you make it. God's word say's a good name is better than all the gold and silver in this world.

For me, not having a father who wasn't present, while I was growing up, made me not really know what courage or loyalty was, nor did I know how to step up and take charge and be a hero. I also was not an example to not only.

My children but to other fatherless children.

CHAPTER ONE

Statistics of a Fatherless Home

Galatians 6:9 So don't get tired of doing what is good. Don't get discouraged and give up, for we will reap a harvest of blessing at the appropriate time

Ephesians 6:4 Fathers do not exasperate your children; Instead, bring them up in the training and Instruction of the Lord (NIV)

AS TIME GOES BY, WE AS FATHERS FIND OURSELVES CONSUMED with financial dilemmas and problems at work. But, the big problem we're facing is the growth of children logging into Facebook, Myspace, Instagram and Snapchat.

We can find our children being lured into this lifestyle of social media, and losing them.

Fathers are not being a major part of their children's' lives, so the children go where they can find love or acceptance, sex, drugs, parties, gangs, and violence, etc.

Children from fatherless homes are more likely to live in poverty, become involved in drug and alcohol abuse, become school dropouts and suffer from emotional problems. Boys are likely to join gangs and adopt a criminal lifestyle. Girls are more likely to become involved in sexual relationships resulting in teen pregnancy. According to the Department of Health and Human Services, children living with only a mother present in the home have a 42.6 percent poverty rate, which is over four times the rate of a married couple, consisting of a husband and a wife.

In 2001, homes without a dad head of household family structure with children 39.2 percent, with both parents 8 percent.

In 2003, without a father 41.7 percent, with both parents 8.6 percent.

Then look at 2011, without a father 47.6 percent. With both parents, 10.9 percent.

Did you know that 71 percent of all high school dropouts come from fatherless homes? Eight-five percent of all youth in prison come from fatherless homes and 90 percent of all homeless and runaway children come from fatherless homes.

Children with both biological parents have significantly fewer externalizing and internalizing behavioral problems than those living with just one non-biological parent.

Children in grades 2 through 12 living with one parent who

is divorced or separated reported a lower grade point average. Children living with their married biological parents had a higher test rate education.

More than 20 million children live in a home without the physical presence of a father. Millions more have dads who are physically present, but emotionally absent.

If it were classified as a disease, fatherlessness would be an epidemic worthy of attention as a national emergency.

An estimated 24.7 million children (33%) live without their biological father. (On a daily basis?)

Of students in grades 1 through 12, 39 percent (17.7 million) live in homes absent their biological fathers.

57.6% of African-American children, 31.2% of Hispanic children, and 20.7% of white children are living absent their biological fathers.

According to 72.2 % of the U.S. population, fatherlessness is the most significant family or social problem facing America.

Children Living with Mother Only

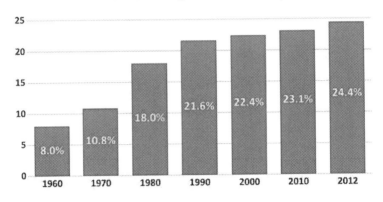

Trended Data

Among children who were part of the "post-war generation," 87.7% grew up with two biological parents who were married to each other. 2017 only 68.1% will spend their entire childhood in an intact family.

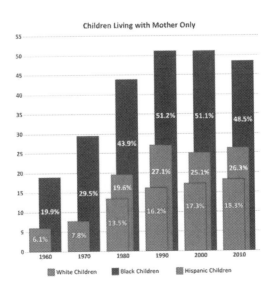

It's time to take back what is lost. Fatherhood needs to return to the way it was meant to be. This is a summary of issues. That are listed below, of some father absence. However it is still a powerful indictment to our current social epidemic. Of individuals raised in a father absent environment.

There is a 5 times the average of suicide rate, a Dramatically increased rate of depression and anxiety, 32 time the average rate of incarceration,

Decreased education levels and increased drop-out rates, Consistently lower average income levels in family, There's a Lower job security, An Increased rates of divorce and relationship issues today, & Substantially increased rate in substance abuse: and a Increases in social and mental behavioral issues in children of a fatherless home.

CHAPTER TWO

My Life Story

WHEN I WAS GROWING UP WITHOUT MY FATHER, I DROPPED OUT of school at age 16. I started drinking and smoking pot. I had a pre-marital sexual relationship and became a father at age 17. Deep inside, I was missing a part of me, of who I was and my identity. In April 1994, I accepted Christ into my heart, mind, spirit and life started to change. I am still learning and growing as a father.

I woke up from hearing my Heavenly Father telling me my children could walk in my footsteps. I then started changing even more…a lot more! I saw a Christian movie called "Courageous" which showed me what a real father is. I realized that I wanted my daughters to love and serve their Heavenly Father. In Exodus 20, it states, "Honor your father and mother." I want my daughters to respect their elders, open doors, help others in need, forgive others, and not to judge based on color or race.

Growing up, I never knew my father, nor did I never met him. I learned as I got older that I was missing something in life, a father figure. I needed someone to show me how to be a man and what a man is, how to treat your wife, how to fix a bike, throw a baseball or football, ride a bike, and show me how to be a father myself. I had a mother that did her best on her own.

As I got older…I was empty…lacking something? I was fatherless. When I got bullied in school and had no one to talk to, I needed a father when my daughters were born, they did not have a grandfather nor did I have a father to teach me, or so I thought.

Until someone told me about my father in heaven, Abba Father (God). God said that when your father and mother forsake you, I will never leave you nor forsake you. I learned in time that God really is a father and He loved me and you so much that he gave his only son for us to live life abundantly. I was learning how to be a husband and still am. I started to learn what love really is and is not according to 1 Corinthians 13.

By not having a father growing up, I saw how important a father is and how he should be. I needed a father. I needed to teach me right from wrong, how to fish, hunt, provide, work hard, to be disciplined and respectful. I needed a dad to go to when I needed a father's advice or how to be man, handling pressure, paying Bills, or fixing a car. I needed a father to show me how a husband lives, behaves and treats a wife. Maybe I would not be divorced twice, or I might have had a better chance, if I had had a father in my life.

It hurt after years to find out who my dad was and then find out that he had died. The night, my cousin, Mark, told me, the anger left. I was delivered. I said, "Dad, I'm sorry I hated you." I cried because I never knew my earthly father but I found my Heavenly Father. I realized I wasn't as good of a father that I thought I was. After watching a Christian movie dealing with being a great father & a book from that movie, I came to realize I needed to make changes. No matter how difficult it was I had to face it head on.

I have decided that I need to change my life style & bad habits, so I can lead by example for my daughters. I needed to encourage them to pray & listen to their heavenly father & read His word

I have found out how to be a great leading father. Today I spend more time with them, plus explain right from wrong plus to treat people how they want to be treated. I know now the role I play in my daughter's life & I must do my very best to lead a upright, one they look up to and be proud of as a father.

Daughters look to us for love support understanding and how a husband treats his wife and fathers his children. If I do my job right my daughters will not settle. I haven't always done or made the right choice in my life for me, but today when God before me no one can be against me. I know I can do all things through Christ who strengthens me. I do and will do my best for my children, teach, show and lead by example.

So I go out of my way to do the most, no matter what I can. I am still working on how to become the father I need to be. I'm still working on bettering my relationship with my children.

On June 21st around 7:30 in the morning, my mother was asleep in her bedroom war fire escape wall was partly gone, and my brother and I were asleep in the living room on our fold out bed. When our building had collapse.

When I woke up all I saw around me was building debris as I was yelling for my brother Dale. This was a terrible day for everyone that lived in the building. A 2 year old girl who I had played with day before had lost her live and seeing her mom yelling for her daughter all I could hear was ware my baby ware my baby. I had miner bruises and my brother had bruises and lost a toe nail.

Accord to the Towanda Police Department they said I should've not survived that day from what my mom told me.

But I guess God had better plains for me instead.

Building Was Not Condemned

By GARRY VANGORDER

TOWANDA — At least two residents of the apartment building here that collapsed and killed a 4-year-old child yesterday had been concerned with the structure's stability since last winter, a published report said this morning.

But despite the concern of William and Sharron Elliott, who allegedly discovered cracks in their bedroom wall and noticed that an outside supporting wall was "bowing out," the building was not condemned — it was simply scheduled for repair work.

Various reports have alleged that 13 persons continued to live in the Wenck apartment building at 12 park St. even after borough officials had condemned it, but neither Towanda building inspector Ambrose Dunn nor borough manager George Snell ever issued such an order.

"There were problems with the exterior of the building," Dunn said yesterday, "and the problem needed immediate repair. I did not feel, however, that condemning the building was necessary.

Billie Jo Yates, daughter of 27-year-old Rosemary Yates, died in the early morning building collapse near the Bradford County Court House. Officials are still investigating the mishap, but indications are that the supporting wall, weakened when a vehicle struck it several weeks ago, gave way and tumbled occupants and rubble into the street.

Seven persons were injured but were eventually released from Towanda Memorial Hospital.

A June 2 order from Dunn to John Wenck, the building's owner, directed the Towanda man to effect repairs to the 110-year-old structure or tear it down. Wenck, in compliance with a borough ordinance, notified Dunn's office within five days that various contractors were studying the work to be done.

It was a contractor who told Wenck that the building's residents would have to leave the premises before repairs could begin. Wenck then notified his tenants that they had two weeks to move. All were to be out of the building by tomorrow.

"They were going to remove the wall and repair it," Snell said this morning. "Unfor-

(Continued on Back Page)

BILLIE JO YATES
a tragic death.

Collapsed Building

The Wenck apartment building in Towanda, which collapsed and killed a 4-year-old girl, had not been officially condemned by borough officials despite the detection of a weakened supporting wall. Although contractors had urged the evacuation of all residents prior to commencement of repair work, the wall gave way early yesterday with 13 persons still living in the structure.

Evening Times Photo — Paluzzi

15

Family Was to Move Today

By GARRY VANGORDER

TOWANDA — A five-year-old girl was killed and six other persons were injured when a supporting wall to their three-story apartment building collapsed at 7:15 this morning.

Dead is Billie Joe Yates, one of 11 persons residing in the Wenck apartment building on Park Street here.

The building, which was not condemned but had been scheduled for repair by owner John (Ted) Wenck, is adjacent to the borough hall and across the street from the Bradford County Court House.

Treated for multiple contusions and released were the dead child's mother, 27-year-old Rosemary Yates, five-year-old Amy Yates, Darlene Yates (age not available), seven-year-old Todd Johnson, 14-year-old Dale Johnson and eight-year-old Penni Elliott.

The Yates girl was pronounced dead at the scene by deputy county coroner Gene Farr. The cause of death has officially been listed as asphyxiation.

The names of those not injured in the mishap were not available at presstime.

According to witnesses at the scene, the building collapsed when the weakened supporting wall gave way.

Towanda building inspector Ambrose Dunn told The Evening Times this morning that the wall, which bordered an alley, was damaged recently when hit by a truck. According to Dunn, Wenck was instructed to begin repairs on the structure after all residents had vacated the premises.

All residents were given two weeks to move from the building and according to Wenck, that deadline was due to expire this week.

The Yates were to move today.

"The building needed immediate attention," Dunn said, "but I didn't think it necessary to condemn the structure.

It has been reported that borough officials had officially condemned the structure as of June 1, and Ambrose said that if that action was taken, "it was taken by someone other than myself."

The wall, which according to one Towanda resident was "bowed out like a violin," had reportedly been shored up to prevent its collapse.

Wenck said he had planned to renovate the building in compliance with Dunn's wishes, but it is now apparent the structure will be razed.

The building had housed a vacant beauty shop on its first floor and apartments on the second and third floors, witnesses said. The Yates lived on the second floor.

According to one relative, the Yates were packing to leave the building at the time of the collapse.

CHAPTER THREE

Fathering Of The Fatherless

A FATHER PUTS HIS FAMILY BEFORE HIMSELF, HIS WILL, DREAMS, needs and wants; He is to teach, guide, help, comforts, provides, protect and lead by example; He respects, encourage. A Father should always lead with courage values morals, Godly wisdom, and prayer.

You may have grown up without a father or may have had a "bad" father. But, I am here to tell you that your Heavenly Father will never leave you, will never give up on you, and will never stop loving you. Your Heavenly Father will not call you names, abuse nor abandon you.

He will show you grace, mercy, love, forgiveness, and compassion, and He will restore your joy and happiness.

I think of the parable of the lost son in Luke 15:11-32. One son asked for his inheritance and moved away. This prodigal, like some of us, blew his inheritance foolishly. The other son stayed home, helped his father and did his job. One day, the prodigal found himself sleeping with pigs. He went home. What happened next is short of a miracle in our day and age. Once the son returned, the father hugged his son and said welcome home by declaring a feast. I watch the news and hear how mothers have killed their children. Children have been thrown away into dumpsters.

Where are the fathers? Children have been sold and abandoned. What is going on with people in this world that they do this when they have fathers themselves? It is time to wake up, Fathers, and do your job better than okay or getting by. I believe we can build up and tear down our families. You might say "how is that?" Simple.

Ephesians 6:4 states "Fathers, do not provoke your children to wrath..." How do we do this? Simple, the actions and words we use towards our wives and children and Co-workers. When we watch what we say and do, we are showing our kids and other kids how a man, husband or father should live, behave, treat others. The book of Proverbs says the tongue speaks life and death.

Our children learn from us and take it into the world, school, church, work and in their families.

So, Fathers, it is time to be a Hebrews' man. What does this mean? To direct, command or order. God chose us men to fatherhood so we need to enable and direct our children in the way they should live, behave, treat others and to make right life choices.

If we do not encourage or direct our children and give them a healthy direction in love, they will find it through their peers, media, culture and other places. Let's be great life-changing mentors and model fathers. After all, we are their first teachers.

I believe if we as fathers would go above and beyond, we can be our children's biggest heroes. I am calling all fathers to be greater, life changers for your children and for children who do not have fathers. It is now time to rise up as men and fathers and take the mantle and run with it at all costs. It is time to respect the role that God passed down to fathers. Lay down your life, pick up your cross and be the fathers that God told and showed you how to be.

We see men of God like Abraham, Moses, Joshua, David and many more in the Old Testament and men like Paul the New Testament pass down their mantel for others to pick up and carry on further.

As fathers, we can learn from these men and pass down to our children and grandchildren the value, morals and respect they need to live a great life. But we must not and cannot take our fatherhood lightly or lying down but must lead by example. By the way we treat and speak to our wives and children, how we act at work, and by teaching and doing as well ourselves, working hard, not complaining, saving and investing.

Treat your wife like a queen, your son like a prince and your daughter like a princess. Take part in what they like and listen to what they have to say is a great start of saying I love you, I care and, most of all, you matter.

Start having Daddy Days for yourself with your Heavenly Father and your earthly dad. And most of all, have and enjoy Daddy Days with your children by tea parties and dress up to throwing a ball, cutting grass or working on cars.

Also, take time with your wife and help around the house. It is good for your children to see their mother and father working together in one accord, side by side. Also let your children see your love for each other with a hug, kiss, holding hands or kind words to each other.

Let's invest in the lives of children today. We can change a generation of fatherless and lack.

Let's be leaders and be mentors.

What a difference one can make to take the time to step out and father a child through mentoring and leading by example. It's time to resurrect fatherhood. It's time to man-up and be the father. Don't give up and run like a selfish child throwing a fit. You and I must be courageous and step up. It's time to stop being afraid or unwilling to mentor other children.

I wonder if fathers realize the role they live out for their children's lives. What an impact it is for them in a mighty way. It makes a big difference in our children's lives in an overall healthy and godly way.

I hope fathers around America will step up or make the call to start over and make the difference so that healing and deliverance can take place.

The book of Psalms and other books of the Holy Bible display and show the love and character of a true father. God is an awesome father. He sees you for who you are, not what you are. He loves you unconditionally and wants to bless you, not curse you and restore all that is lost and broken.

CHAPTER FOUR

Adoption by God

F.A.M.I.L.Y

Finding a Meaning Inside Loving You

Deuteronomy 10:18 "He defends the cause of the fatherless and the widow; and loves the foreigner residing among you, giving them food and clothing"

As Hebrew & Gentile fathers, we must keep watch, be on guard and observe our children's surroundings. Through a relationship with our Heavenly Father, we can learn to relate with God's righteousness We can learn to love as a father in a way that our own children will look up to us and follow our footsteps, passing down to their own children. We can change a town, community, state, and country. Self-sacrifice is what makes it worthwhile to our parenthood. So, it's time to father-up and lead by example.

Raise the bar to emulate our Heavenly Father in love, forgiveness, mercy and understanding, our children blame or believe it is their fault that their fathers left, gave up and abandoned them and their families.

Throughout the Bible, we can find what and who a father is and is not. It is time to read, research, think apply and act it out now, not tomorrow. In God's word, He makes a number of statements towards children without fathers that are not in the home or have left because they did not care. Such as "when your father and mother forsake you, I will not.

> Zechariah 7:10 "do not oppress the widow or the fatherless, the foreigner or the poor. Do not plot evil against each other" (NIV).

Your Heavenly Father makes it clear. He will never leave you, abandon you, give up or stop loving you. God showed this to the Israelites' for 40 years by supplying manna and a pillar of fire to guide them at night and clouds by day. Your Heavenly Father loves you so much. He said He will finish what he started plus He would bless those who bless you and curse those who curse you. If you read the Bible and ask "what about me, where do I fit in?" First of all you were made by God for a purpose. Second, you were made in His image and likeness. When God gave His only son, Jesus, to die on the cross, that day, over 2,000 years ago, God adopted you into the family of Heaven.

You always have a father in this world that will love you unconditionally in heaven. God who made you in his image knows every part of you. He loves and values everything about you and the things in your life so much that His son gave His life for you. God is a type of father you can go to share your deepest thoughts and secrets. You don't have to feel like you alone are unloved and unwanted, because you have a father that will always be by your side.

God said you have an inheritance in Heaven. You became joint heirs of Christ Jesus and a child of God the day you said "Jesus, come in to my heart and fix what's broken, heal what's sick, restore what's lost," mending your spirit, heart and mind.

From here in your daily journey through reading the Bible and being part of a church family, you grow in your family and through prayer, you are able to speak to your Father.

You can see in Matthew 6:33 and 7:7-12 how God is as a Father when you read His word and through its teaching of living and mentoring the way a father should. Psalm 18:2 "The Lord is my Rock, my Fortress and my Deliverer. My God is my Rock, in whom I take refuge. He is my shield and the horn of my salvation, my stronghold." From these scriptures, we get a sense of a father's love.

What we will and can find in our Heavenly Father. You

fathers, are you ready to step up? Stand out and take your responsibility to be your children's refuge and stronghold? I hope so, your children are a blessing and gift from your Heavenly Father. Don't waste or blow it.

Psalm 1: This chapter tells us how we should be and live. We can learn from this chapter and show our children by example on how to live a righteous life.

> John 3:16 For God so loved the world, he gave his
> only begotten son that whosoever believes in Him
> shall not perish but have ever lasting life."

I hope all of you who never had a father while growing up, like me, can learn, see and feel your Heavenly Father's spirit.

As men, we need to face our problems and fight evil with good. We men must support each other (iron sharpens iron). Once you know and understand what a man really is, you can start learning and being father like, a man accepts his responsibilities and follows through. We must lead and be courageous, preserving through it all and coming out better than the day you became a man and a father.

We, as fathers, not only need to be living examples in our

own children's lives but also in the lives of other children of our churches, schools and communities. It's time to take back our roles as fathers.

The best way to do this is through our Heavenly Father's word. Seek Him out and get to know Him. Then share with your sons and daughters what you learned, passing it down.

If we would Just understanding God as our Father and accepting his deep love & care for you could be helpful, life changing or hindered by experiences with our earthly father's. Has your family relationships played a part in forming or influenced your acceptance of God's love & forgiveness as paternal? For the next generation? We must make better choices and examples for them as God does for us daily.

CHAPTER FIVE

Time To Lead

Ephesians 5 verses 1-20 (NIV)

1 Follow God's example, therefore, as dearly loved children

2 and walk in the way of love, Just as Christ loved us and gave himself up for us as a fragrant offering and sacrifice to God.

3 But among you there must not be even a hint of sexual immorality, or of any kind of impurity, or of greed, because these are improper for God's holy people.

4 Nor should there be obscenity, foolish talk or coarse joking, which are out of place, but rather thanksgiving.

5 For of this you can be sure: No immoral, impure or greedy person—such a person is an idolater— has any inheritance in the kingdom of Christ and of God. **6** Let no one deceive you with empty words, for because of such things God's wrath comes on those who are disobedient.

7 Therefore do not be partners with them.

8 For you were once darkness, but now you are light in the Lord. Live as children of light.

9 (for the fruit of the light consists in all goodness, righteousness and truth).

10 and find out what pleases the Lord.

11 Have nothing to do with the fruitless deeds of darkness, but rather expose them.

12 It is shameful even to mention what the disobedient do in secret.

13 But everything exposed by the light becomes visible—and everything that is illuminated becomes a light.

14 This is why it is said:

"Wake up, sleeper, rise from the dead, and Christ will shine on you."

15 Be very careful, then, how you live—not as unwise but as wise.

16 making the most of every opportunity, because the days are evil.

17 Therefore do not be foolish, but understand what the Lord's will is.

18 Do not get drunk on wine, which leads to debauchery. Instead, be filled with the Spirit,

19 speaking to one another with psalms, hymns, and songs from the Spirit. Sing and make music from your heart to the Lord,

20 always giving thanks to God the Father for everything, in the name of our Lord Jesus Christ.

JOSHUA 24:15 As FOR ME & MY HOUSE WE WILL SERVE THE LORD I have decided to love my children & protect them & teach them the word of God as there spiritual & earthly dad & leader of their house. I have read God calls the most unlikely to become great men as he did for Abraham, Moses & Joshua. Like these men God can & will lead you and equip you with all you need spiritual to grow, learn, & lead your family with greatness.

> Romans 6:23 "The wages of sin is death, but the free gift of God is eternal life in Christ Jesus our Lord"

God has given me authority to do what he has laid before us to do. He gave us His word to meditate day & night to make us prosperous in all our endeavors and help us succeed as men and leaders of our homes.

We also have His presence through the Holy Spirit to be our companion, helper and guide to shield us.

Men as fathers we cannot sleep on our watch. We cannot just high tail away from our responsibilities and give up and walk away, but it's time to pick up your cross follow Jesus, and be the leader of your home, teach love, guide, forgive, & help us.

Cherish your children lead them to greatness, build them up, encourage them. The sky is the limit and show them how proud you are there dad.

> Psalms 127:3 "Children are a gift from the Lord:
> They are reward from Him."

Be a loving & living example be willing to make the first move, praying, before bed hug, kiss, or just listening to your children. As fathers & husbands of the house or single fathers, we must lay down our life and will for the ones we love and been given to cherish and take care of under your care.

The more we as fathers humble ourselves and serve our family good hearted and sacrificially you will become more Gods way and should be your way as well. The old and new testaments commission dads to train up their children in the ways of God and they should go to become spiritual successful and spiritual wise and understanding.

Deuteronomy 6:7-9 "Repeat them again and again to your children. Talk about them when you are at home and when you are away on a journey, when you are laying down and when you are getting up again. Tie them to your hands as reminder, and wear them ion your forehead. Write them on the door posts of your house and on your gates. It is time fathers to take the call and re-engage and be courageous enough to help make the changes you need. It might not happen overnight, but it is under your watch. I have read a number of books and I learned we must not waste our time, we can't play the blame game, but instead immediately get involved leading our children with a purpose, deal with the problem head on & fix it.

To prevent problems from happening again.

> Colossians 3:21 "Fathers, don't aggravate your children, if you do, they become discouraged and quit trying"

For me I am doing all I can to do my very best to be the father God called me to be. It's hard at times, but I have to overcome and say it's not my will or about me, but it's for my children's well-being & spiritual well-being. I go out of my way to do what I must no matter what I can. I am still learning how to become the father I need to be.

Even though at times it feels hard or a lost cause it is our jobs as fathers to emulate the character of the unconditional love and discipline to our children as our heavenly father does with us.

So our sons and daughters will grow to learn the true love and respect values and morals of their heavenly father through us, as earthly fathers.

This may sound easier said than done or even hard to do. As I have found out for myself as a father trying to reconnect and restore my relationships with my children. I have found out that our children will do the things we have done in our lives and their own. We must be passionate and make better choices as fathers so this way they make better choices in their lives. We must practice what we teach or tell our children we must value listening, care, love everything about them. Making time to listen to them to help them grow and learn in love.

We must be diligent never leaving them, so make sure you spend time with your children so they know they are valued and cared about. It is vital that children know that are the apple of their fathers eye.

We as men & fathers are God's Bearer's. We are to accept our fatherhood, responsibilities as fathers. Function in our behavior likewise as we would have our children behave.

1 Corinthians 13:4 "Love is patient, love is kind. It doesn't envy does not boast it is not proud." (NIV)

1Corinthians 16:14 "Do everything in love." (NIV)

1 Corinthians 13:6 "Love doesn't delight in evil but rejoices with the truth." (NIV)

Pray to God to give you the strength to follow through with your duties as a Father.

Scripture to study 2 Chronicles 30:7-9

Where there is any sin, bitterness, lies repent and break the chain of your Fathers.

Notes: _____

_____

_____

_____

_____

_____

_____

_____

_____

_____

At this very moment in time we as fathers have a key role through prayer and the voice of God to play a key role in our children life to release them in to their adult identity. Since our key role as fathers, we are to minister blessings to our children daily.

When we as fathers miss the opportunity to bless our children we can still take the place at a later time to realizes there need's.

"Even if you don't see immediate results in serving your children when trying to rebuild your relationship, we have faith that God will bring the results and change in them over time and we Father's might change a generation who will be great men and Fathers of God & dance, smile and sing again!"

CHAPTER SIX

Psychological Aspects of Fatherlessness Home

FATHERING THE FATHERLESS

ACCORDING TO TWO ARTICLES I READ BY MICHAEL KISMET and Gina Scott Fatherlessness is a serious problem we live with into adult hood till we get help.

I personally never knew I'd have any psychological or mental behavior issues growing up, until I started my first book. I wrote Fathering The Fatherless, through research II found. I started seeing in my life I had a lot of anger Issues, problems paying attention, not focusing, not getting along well with others. I have found threw research on line that anger, depression, suicide, tolerance of abuse, behavioral problems are just some of the psychological effects of Fatherlessness in the family home. It can have a great impact on who we become later in life and how we live. Psychological ramifications of growing up fatherless can have serious problems.

I myself personally experienced many psychological consequences mentioned in articles. Growing without a father could and might permanently alter the structure of the brain. Did you notice it said "permanently"? Growing up in a single parent home, I found it can be difficult in life.

Psychological studies show that children growing up without their father are more likely to be aggressive and quick to get angry. The most common psychological effect of fatherlessness is feeling angry. Typically at the very core of the anger is pain, rejection and hurt.

It stems from the rejection felt from loved ones. It varies in forms such as verbal outbursts, cutting their body, and physical violence. Due to the psychological various behavioral problems, depression and suicide subsequently are very unfortunate dealing with the absent of their dad in their life and home.

Children must learn how to cope with their sadness of an absent father. The state of fatherlessness in the world has a psychologically side effect on all the young people as they grow up and forum there personal own identities.

According to P.L. Adams J.R. Milner when the father is absent from the home boys have a problem with establishing appropriate sex roles and gender identity. There is a greater risk for children without their father in the home have a greater risk of suicide. (Us department of health and human services) emotional distress is a part of the mental thought process children living with a never married mother are more likely to be treated for emotional issues.

According to the co-sponsored by the National Association

Elementary School Principals and the Charles F. Kettering foundation. It states children with both parents in the home tend to do better in school, are less prone to depression and are more successful in relationships than those without both parents.

Children with one parent get in more trouble and have more problems than those who have both parents. The numbers of statistics of problems children have with no father in the home. So as we can see it is very important as fathers to do your very best to train and raise up your children right in unconditional love always.

Lead by example every day and let's end fatherlessness together.

CHAPTER SEVEN

Testimonies Of Men Stepping Up As Fathers

FATHERING THE FATHERLESS

PROVERBS 3:1-8

1 My child, never forget the things I have taught you. Store my commands in your heart.

2 for they give you a long and satisfying life.

3 Never let loyalty and kindness get away from you! Wear them like a necklace, write them deep within your heart.

4 Then you will find favor with both God and people, and you will gain a good reputation.

5 Trust in the Lord with all your heart, do not depend on your own understanding,

6 Seek His will in all you do, and He will direct your paths.

Don't be impressed with your own wisdom. Instead, fear the Lord and turn your back on evil.

8 Then you will gain renewed health and vitality.

I SPOKE TO A COLLEAGUE OF MINE FROM WORK WHO HAS GONE above and beyond a dads duties.

This is Kevin's story as he puts it.

I have mentored kids for quite a while, less officially early on as I would help or council kids needing guidance via friends or others. When I met my current wife she came with two boys who I must now know as my sons, taking them in and on, so to speak. Also leading to my stint as Boy Scout leader.

Through all of that I have found that kids need a lot of love and guidance and sometimes just someone to show them things that they have no exposure to.

I have shared working on cars/trucks, electronics, music, canoeing, camping, and even the use of hot glue guns with kids through the years.

More recently our adoption of Eden began as emergency placement as her home had become unsafe, taking her in what was the only right thing we could do and she has won us over with her charm and appreciation of simple things, she has been through a lot... way more than any kid should.. But she always has a smile and a hug ready.

The impact I hope that parenting kids and mentoring them

has helped them be well rounded, educated, happy, and have all of their needs met. I enjoy sharing things that are special or unique to me with them seeing them grow in those areas.

The boys have told me they appreciate me being a real dad and having some common sense and raising them. My scouts were always super grateful to have exposure to things even if they were not fatherless in reality, Eden does not yet speak much but in her own way she demonstrates how much being loved and cared for means to her every day.

Many of the kids in the past were grateful for a listening ear and big heart as they would say. More than what they say kids whether my own, adopted, mentored etc. All respond to having some fatherly input, they begin to thrive and reciprocate the care you give.

From National Center for Fathering Watch D.O.G.S.

According to department of health and human services

Todd Johnson Frazee, Minnesota

INDEX SOURCES

U<small>NLESS</small> <small>OTHERWISE</small> <small>STATED</small> <small>ALL</small> BIBLE S<small>CRIPTURE</small> REFRENCESS COME FROM NEW KING JAMES & New International Version.

STATISTICS OF FATHERLESS COMES FROM

- Source: U.S. Census Bureau. "Living Arrangements of Children Under 18 Years Old: 1960 to Present". U.S. Census Bureau July 1, 2012.

    HTTP://www.census.gov/popul action/so demo/hh-fam/ch5.xls

- Source: U.S. Census Bureau. "Living Arrangements of Children Under 18 Years Old: 1960 to Present". U.S. Census Bureau July 1, 2012.

    http://www.census.gov/populati on/socdemo/hh-fam/ch5.xls

- Children Living with Mother Only graph.qxd

- Source: Census Bureau. "Living Arrangements of Children Under 18 Years Old: 1960 to Present." U.S. Census Bureau, July 1, 2012.

http://www.census.gov/population/socdemo/hh-fam/
ch5.xls

- Source: Popenoe, David. Life Without Father (New York: Simon and Schuster, 1996), 23.

- Source: US Census Bureau, "Living Arrangements of Children under 18": Tables – CH-2, CH-3, CH-4. 1960 – Present. U.S. Census Bureau July 1, 2012.This information comes from National Center for Fathering Watch D.O.G.S.

  Source: US Census Bureau, "Living Arrangements of Children Under 18": Tables –CH-2, CH-3, CH-4. 1960 – Present. U.S.

  Census Bureau July 1, 2012.

  This information comes from National Center for Fathering Watch D.O.G.S.

- Source: Nord, Christine Winquist, and Jerry West. Fathers' and Mothers' Involvement in their Children's Schools by Family Type and Resident Status. Table 1. (NCES 2001-032).

Washington, DC: U.S. Dept. of Education, National Center of Education Statistics, 2001.

- Source: National Center for Fathering, Fathering in America Poll, January, 1999

  Newspaper articals are from The Daily Review or other paper out lits in Towanda.

SCRIPTURE INDEX TO STUDY TO BETTER YOUR FATHER HOOD!

1 Corinthians13:4 "Love is patient, love is kind. It doesn't envy does not boast it is not proud." (NIV)

1 Corinthians16:14 "Do everything in love." (NIV)

1 Corinthians13:6 "Love does delight in evil but rejoices with the truth." (NIV)

Colossians 3:21 "Fathers, don't aggravate your children, if you do, they become discourage and quite trying"

Ephesians 6:4 Father's do not exasperate your children; Instead, bring them up in the training and instruction of the Lord

1 Corinthians 16:13
Genesis 1:26 & 2:15

Genesis 2:24 1 Timothy 3:4-5

Genesis 2:24 1 Timothy 3:4-5
1 Corinthians 15:58

1) How does one lead as a father by

Example:

_____

_____

_____

_____

_____

2) How can you know you are fathered by God your Heavenly

   Father:

_____

_____

_____

_____

_____

3) As children how can they know their father love's them:

_____

_____

_____

_____

_____

4) When is it a good time for healing and deliverance to start:

_____

_____

_____

_____

_____

5) What word best describe the way you lead as a father:

_____

_____

_____

_____

_____

6) In what way can you show yourself as a good model of a good father:

_____

_____

_____

_____

_____

7) Is there anything in your life that you are reluctant to find

out that God wants to do through you as a father or father

to be:

_____

_____

_____

_____

_____

8) How do you define Fatherhood:

_____

_____

_____

_____

_____

9) What are some things that keep you or have kept you as a father to act like a father should:

_____

_____

_____

_____

_____

10) What are some signs that would show there is fatherlessness:

_____

_____

_____

_____

_____

I hope this book has been helpful & eye opening to something that should never be or ever have happened FATHERLESSNESS!!!!!!!!!!!!!!!!!!

SO please rebuild your relationships with your children learn to forgive and lead by God's example from now on....

Father God I ask that you be my father, to show and teach me as a father should teach its child in Jesus name.

Father God help me to restore mend and rebuild my relationship with my children or child in Jesus name to be and become the Father that you are as I am to be amen.

ABOUT THE AUTHOR

Todd R Johnson has been a resident of Frazee MN. For over 10 years. He's been a member at Harvest Fellowship Church (Frazee, MN) for 8 years. Todd attended Vineyard Church of (Detroit Lakes, MN), and Assemblies of God (Pelican Rapids, MN) where he was in charge of ushers, greeters and the event coordinator. Todd has attended Calvary Evangelical Free Church (Pelican Rapids, MN) Todd has four wonderful daughters and a son. He was a founder of D.O.C. Ministries. Todd was born in Niagara Falls, NY on April 12, 1973. He grew up in Towanda, PA, and various cities in Florida. Todd has volunteered as a teacher's aide for Release Time at his local church.

Printed in the United States
By Bookmasters